21 NOV 2008

0 9 MAR 2010

2 6 MAY 2010

1 3 MAR 2013

- 4 MAR 2015
8 MAR 2016
2 8 JUL 2022

2 8 JUL 2022

Suffolk
County Council

Please return/renew this item
by the last date shown.
Books may also be renewed by
phone or the Internet.

Libraries & Heritage
www.suffolkcc.gov.uk/libraries/

SUFFOLK COUNTY COUNCIL	
07046798	
Bertrams	30.01.08
	£4.95
160075	

Acknowledgements

Photographs © Newspress

Copyright © Axis Education 2007

First published in Great Britain by Axis Education Ltd

ISBN 978-1-84618-091-0

Axis Education
PO Box 459
Shrewsbury
SY4 4WZ

Email: enquiries@axiseducation.co.uk

www.axiseducation.co.uk

Printed by The Cromwell Press, Trowbridge, Wiltshire.

This is a fast car.

It is a Porsche 911.

The first one came out in 1964.

It is called a 2+2.

Porsche 911.

You say 911 like 'nine eleven'.

Porsche is a German company.

It has made cars since 1931.

Porsche was founded by Ferdinand Porsche.

He also made the first Volkswagen.

A classy car.

The Porsche Carrera is a 911 model.

It came out in 1972.

It had a bigger engine than the first 911.

It had a spoiler.

It was lighter than the first 911.

A lighter car.

A modern Carrera is not cheap.

It can cost as much as £80,000.

The fastest Carrera can get from 0 to 60 miles per hour in 4.6 seconds.

That is the same as 0 to 100 kilometres per hour.

It can go as fast as 182mph.

That is 293kph.

It can go 293 kilometres per hour.

The Turbo came out in 1975.

It was also called the Porsche 930.

It had wide wheels.

It had a large spoiler.

This was called a 'Whale Tail' or a 'Tea Tray'.

A car with a tea tray!

The Turbo was also a racing car.

It raced at Le Mans.

It raced until the 1980s.

Many people wanted the Turbo.

Lots of types were made.

They were very expensive.

A racing car.

A modern Porsche 911 Turbo is very expensive.

It costs about £90,000.

It can get from 0 to 60mph in 3.7 seconds.

This is the same as 0 to 100kph.

It can go up to 193mph.

This is the same as 310kph.

0 to 60mph in 3.7 seconds.

Up to 193mph.

Turbo style!

The Porsche GT3 is a two-seater.

It is a light 911 model.

It is a new Porsche.

It costs about £95,000.

The GT3 can get from 0 to 62mph in 4.3 seconds.

It can get from 0 to 100mph in 8.7 seconds!

A modern car.

The modern 911 has good handling.

It has sharp steering.

Many owners think it has the best supercar steering.

The driver has control.

It is easy to drive around bends.

You can really feel the car.

It has sharp steering.

The gear box has six speeds.

It is a new gear box design.

It is smoother than earlier models.

The 911 is smart and fast.

The engine sounds rich.

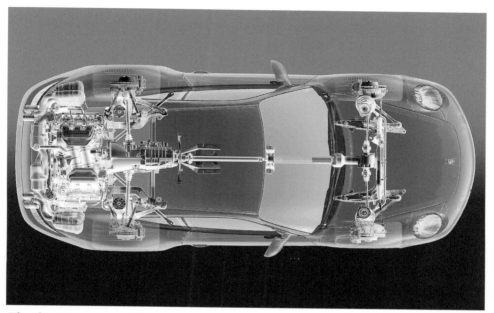

The best supercar?

You sit low in the Porsche 911.

You can move the steering wheel.

There is room in the centre and in the doors.

As the engine is in the boot, there is luggage space under the bonnet.

You can get your holiday bags in it.

A car with space.

There is not much room in the back.

Good vision out of the windows makes up for that.

The seats are comfy.

Porsche will make seats that fit you.

You can have backrests put in for you.

They are electric and hug your body.

An x-ray picture of the 911.

A car for today.

Good vision!

The 911 is not cheap to run.

You might get about 26 miles per gallon out of it.

The insurance is high.

It has six air bags.

It has an alarm and immobiliser.

It is also a race car.

The 911 is also a race car.

The Porsche 911 is a cool car.

It looks great on the road.

It is still a favourite for Porsche lovers.

The design is perfect.

It is classic.

It looks like a Porsche!

Definitely a Porsche!

The 911 has been around for over 40 years.

It has a long history.

There are over 50 different models.

They are all supercars.

40 years of the Porsche 911.

You know a Porsche when you see one.

It is easy to spot.

The design is stylish.

It will live forever.

Easy to spot.

Technical specification – Porsche 911

Make	Porsche
Model	911
Engine size	3600cc
Top speed	190mph (306kph)
Acceleration	0 to 62mph (0 to 100kph) in 4.2 seconds
Fuel tank capacity	64 litres
Price	£90,360
Weight	1540kg
Transmission	6-speed manual/ 5-speed auto
Wheelbase	2350mm

Glossary

acceleration	how fast the car speeds up
backrest	the part of the seat that supports your back
capacity	how much petrol the engine can hold
cc (cubic centimetres)	a measure of engine capacity
favourite	the one you like best
handling	the way the car drives
immobiliser	something that stops anyone starting your car without your keys
insurance	you pay this so that you don't have to pay for repairs if your car is stolen or you have a crash
kg (kilogram)	a measure of weight (just over two pounds)
kph	kilometres per hour
litre	a measure of liquid (just under two pints)
mm (millimetre)	a small measure of length: 10mm = 1cm (centimetre)
mph	miles per hour

per	for every
racing car	a Formula 1 car, for example
rear	the back of the car
spoiler	a fixture on the back of the car that makes it go faster through wind
stylish	classy; looks good
transmission	another word for gearbox
wheelbase	the distance between the front and rear wheels